Buy to Let Property Investing

How I do it

Matthew Wickham

ISBN: 9798590320295

Disclaimer

The advice provided in this publication is general advice only. It has been prepared without taking into account your objectives, financial situation or investment needs. Before acting, you should consider the appropriateness of the advice, having regard to your own objectives, financial situation and investment needs. To the maximum extent permitted by law, the author and publisher disclaim all responsibility, and liability to any person, arising directly or indirectly from any person taking or not taking action, based on the information in this publication. The author and publisher do not provide formal legal, investment, mortgage loan, tax, financial or accountancy advice and any information within this publication should be qualified with a professional.

For Sarah and Ben

Contents

Introduction

Firstly, I would like to thank you for purchasing this book. This is the short, to the point book that I wish had been available before I started investing in Buy to Let property in the UK, in 2013. Over the past 8 years, I have bought a portfolio of multiple properties throughout the UK, starting with my student debt and subsequently overcome the many challenges facing property investors during this time. Buy to Let (B2L) is probably the most well known strategy for investing in property in the UK and is generally considered a low risk strategy that works time and time again. B2L is simple and uncomplicated when executed correctly and given the increasing economic uncertainties in this country and around the world, I have written this book to help those who are considering property investment and want to know how to actually start and thrive in a fast changing economic climate. If I had to start all over again, these are the important factors that I would consider.

Be under no illusion, buying investment property and building a portfolio requires hard work, time and money. Each factor is always required but the extent of each is directly proportional to the other. For example, if you are fortunate enough to have plenty of cash, it is possible to employ other peoples' time and effort rather than use your own. The reverse is also possible and others have written comprehensively on the subject. However, the good news is that investing in Buy to Let property does not require any professional education or qualification, but persistence and consistency will generate increased wealth and create an *almost* passive income over time. To demonstrate this, here is how I do it.

There are effectively two ways to profit from B2L property investment. The first is from rental income and the second is from capital gain on the value of the property. Identifying how much importance an investor wishes to place on each income stream at the start, will help direct the most tax efficient structure for your B2L portfolio. As of 2020, there are advantages in utilising a Limited Company structure when building a property investment portfolio. This is certainly the case for higher income tax payers within the UK and as I am still working as a doctor, it is through my company that I now purchase investment property to hold for the long term. The benefits include a lower rate of corporation tax (18%) compared to personal income tax (40+%), more flexibility from commercial mortgage lenders and no capital gains tax requirements. There are however, increased accounting costs as well as slightly higher lending fees for mortgages and any dividends (greater than £2000) are subject to income tax on withdrawing the money from the company.

There is no right or wrong way to start a property portfolio, but being aware of the implications is important. If you are unsure as to whether you want to be a landlord, it maybe worthwhile buying an investment property personally and seeing how it goes, as the costs of setting up and running a Limited Company will probably not be viable for a single buy to let property. If however, you are sure that you want to start a property portfolio with the ambition to grow beyond 4 properties, then a Limited Company structure is likely to be a more profitable option. Setting up a Limited company is straightforward and takes less than 30 minutes online at https://www.gov.uk/limited-company-formation/register-your-company. It costs £12 to incorporate a new company and it is possible to register a new company with HMRC at the same time. It would be prudent to make sure you seek personal, professional accounting advice prior to starting any property investment company.

Get to know your Area

Ideally, I would invest close to where I live, as this is the area where I already know the good streets (or not so good streets!) and already know the sort of values that houses sell and rent for. If you are fortunate enough to live somewhere where it is immediately obvious that the house prices are wildly high compared to rents, then you may need to focus on another area a bit further away. Generally, but not exclusively, it is easier to find higher rental yields in the North of England and Scotland versus higher capital growth in the South of England. I cannot stress how important this is - **the better you know an area, the better your investment purchase will be**.

I mainly invest in the West of Scotland, as I live in Glasgow and typically find rental property with at least 10% gross yields (Gross Yield = Annual Gross Rent / Purchase Price) but accept that capital growth is a bonus when it occurs. To get an estimate for any area, compare similar types and sizes of property that are for sale and for rent on sites like Rightmove and Zoopla. Speaking (in person or via Social Media) with local agents and other investors in any specific area will also give you valuable local information. There really is no better way to identify a suitable area for buy to let investing.

Who is your Tenant?

Once you have found the area, we need to identify who the target tenant demographic is:

- Professional / Employed
- Universal Credit
- Housing Benefit
- Students
- Asylum Seekers
- Corporate (Businesses / Charities etc)

This is useful to know before looking at any potential properties, as different tenant types have different expectations. For example, students will expect furnished properties as well as bills included in some regions. I have a contract with the government contractor for asylum seekers to stay in one of my properties and this states that the property will be maintained within a reasonable state of repair for the duration of the agreement. This includes their responsibility to manage the tenants as well as resolve ongoing maintenance repairs within the property. This results in less expenditure, no management fees and no void periods for the duration of the contract (can be up to 5 years), hence increased profits.

Differing tenant expectation costs (furnished or unfurnished, bills included etc.) must be factored into your calculations as part of the buying process. Interestingly, with the COVID-19 pandemic, those tenants that are paid Universal Credit or Housing Benefits have been able to pay their rents throughout this period of uncertainty. Local Housing Authority rates are usually easy to find on each councils website to give an indication of the likely rent achieved.
In my experience, a good tenant will usually stay in the property for longer, regardless of the means which they use to pay their rent. The cashflow calculation formulae (below) can help decide if the property is going to provide an acceptable level of return, based on the specific type and size of property for your target tenant market. We shall see a worked example in the next chapter.

Cashflow Formulae:

Where a letting agent is used, a rate of 10% + VAT is assumed. (Currently VAT is payable at 20%)
Assuming a Limited Company Ownership, all Mortgage Interest is deductible and Corporation Tax of 19% applicable.

Cashflow = Rent (yr) - Total Costs (yr)

Costs Include:

(S) Safety Certificates (Gas / Electric)

(I) Insurance (Buildings / Contents / Rent / Landlord)

(L) Licensing fees

(Gr) Ground rents

(Bm) Building Management / Factor Fees

(M) Maintenance costs (Assume 5% of total rent)

(V) Void periods (2 weeks per year = 3.85% of total rent)

(Mc) Mortgage costs (Interest only)

(Lf) Letting fees (Initial Setup of tenancy)

Self Managed B2L

Cashflow = (0.9115 x Rent) - (S + I + L + Gr + Bm + Mc)

Fully Managed B2L

Cashflow = (0.7915 x Rent) - (S + I + L + Gr + Bm + Mc + Lf)

Profit Formula

Profit = 0.81 x (Cashflow - Accountant Fees - Other Allowable Business Expenses)

Finding a Property

Until this point, it is prudent to do the above steps yourself, as it will be your property investment and you are the key decision maker. Outsourcing the above will only lead to indecision and confusion. Thankfully, it is possible to automate or even completely outsource how to find the property to buy. Online is the obvious place to start (Rightmove, Zoopla, OnTheMarket etc). It is possible to setup specific searches that automatically email you when a property that meets your criteria (area, house, flat, size, condition, price etc) is listed for sale. Ideally, you can do your own research on the property before arranging to view it. Check if its in a flood region, what was the previous sale price as well as current comparable sale prices in that street/area (Rightmove Sold / Land registry). NB if you search the land registry, there is usually a small fee, but it is the most accurate source.

Below is an example of how to assess a potential B2L property.

An ex-local authority, 2 bed flat (freehold) in Glasgow with an asking price of offers over £60,000 and a home report RICS valuation of £63,000. (Uniquely, in Scotland, the Seller has to supply the Home Report Survey prior to listing on the open market.)

The home report survey is satisfactory and no major structural or internal issues are highlighted.

The EPC (Energy Performance Certificate) rating is C, which is useful as there are planned changes to ensure that homes in the UK are at least a C from 2025 onwards.

There is a property factor responsible for the maintenance an communal upkeep for the building which is from the private arm of the local council. Previous experience with this factor is that they are reasonably priced at ~£150/quarter. This could be confirmed by simply asking the estate agent prior to any viewing.

The property was listed with an online estate agent and this potentially gives us direct access to the current owner of the property as they often do the viewings themselves to save on selling costs. This is advantageous if you are looking to buy with any discount as you can make your offer directly to the owner.

This is in essence a potential turnkey investment property. It would be unlikely that any money would need to be spent prior to rental and maintenance costs would be reasonably low also.

Onto the rental aspects - the Local Housing Authority rate for a 2 bed property is £149.59 per week.

This is equivalent to £648 pcm or £7,778 per yr.

Comparable 2 bed properties are available for rent at values of £660 pcm and £700 pcm in the same area.

Financial Considerations:

Purchase Price	£63,000
Deposit of 25%	£15,750
Tax (LBTT at 4%)	£2,520

Solicitor	£850
Broker and Mtg Fees	£850
Total Capital Investment	**£19,970**
Rent	£7,778 / year
Mortgage (4% Interest only)	£1,890 / year
Management Fee (12%) (Equivalent to 10% + VAT)	£933.36 / year
Factor Fee	£600 / year
Insurance (Estimated)	£150 / year
Gas Safety Certificate	£60 / year
EICR (5 yearly at £125)	£25 / year
Maintenance (5%)	£388.90 / year
Net Cashflow	£3,730.74 / year

Profit (Assuming 19% Corporation Tax)	£3,021.90 / year or £251.82 pcm
Return on Investment (ROI)	15.1% (3,021.9/19,970)

For this calculation, I am deliberately assuming a limited company purchase, with no discount on the purchase price and using the LHA rate of rental income which is slightly lower than the private rental options. I have also included a rate of management fee at 12% (equivalent to 10% + VAT) and included a modest budget for repairs, even though the property is reportedly in good order. No calculation of capital appreciation of the property is considered as this is not a readily quantifiable amount. Any capital appreciation would be considered a bonus. As such, this calculation shows the lower estimate of return and therefore gives a good indication of what is achievable prior to even viewing the property. I find this to be a useful exercise before spending any time on viewings. By using a reputable letting agent, the risk of managing the tenant, whether they are private or LHA is significantly reduced and therefore not a deciding factor at this stage of the research process.

If the worst case numbers as above, are still acceptable levels of return on investment, then its worth proceeding to actually view the property and make an offer after the viewing.

It is however, possible to instruct another person (a Property Sourcer) to find a suitable investment property and secure the agreed sale on your behalf. This type of service usually has a fee between £2000 - £3000 per buy to let property, but removes all the time required to actually view and offer on multiple properties as well as finding a property with a discounted price. Being knowledgable about the area and specific in your investment requirements, enable you to confidently assess the information provided by any property sourcer. If you are interested to find out more about property sourcer's, check out the free blog that I have written at https://www.wickhamproperty.co.uk/blog/Introductiontopropertysourcing where you will also find contact information for property sourcer's across the whole of the UK.

Purchasing the Property

Once a purchase price has been agreed, the legal conveyancing process can begin. If it is a cash purchase, this process can be a fast as 2 weeks, but if a mortgage is required, I would anticipate at least 12 weeks before the purchase is complete. There are slight differences between the English and Scottish Legal systems, but the fundamentals of the conveyancing process are the same. For a typical B2L purchase, I would anticipate legal costs and relevant search fees to be roughly £1000.

The assistance of a knowledgable B2L mortgage broker is invaluable at this stage.

Applying for a B2L mortgage to purchase an investment property is probably more straightforward than obtaining a mortgage for your own home. It is possible to obtain a B2L mortgage before buying your own home, but beware the impact of Additional Dwelling Supplement (ADS) which is 3% additional Stamp Duty Tax on the purchase price when buying a second property (4% additional LBTT in Scotland and Wales). Note that for properties under the value of £40,000, ADS is not applicable.

Below is a generic guide, based on my own experience with B2L mortgage lenders:

- Lenders will take the expected rental income into account when assessing affordability. Each lender has there own way of stress testing the rent calculation in relation to the interest payable on the mortgage. As such, it is often beneficial to apply for Interest Only mortgages, as this helps to meet the lending criteria.

- Portfolio landlords are defined as those who own 4 or more rented properties. Lenders often want to know about the whole portfolio before lending on any new purchase. Interest repayment stress tests are then applied to the whole portfolio.

- It is possible to have multiples of B2L mortgages in a portfolio. Some lenders restrict the number of properties they will lend on, others do not.

- The majority of lenders want to see that you have some income from another source (i.e. not rental income) on your initial application (usually £25,000 gross earnings) but there are lenders who do not necessarily require this.

- Expect to pay at least a 20% deposit, but in most cases 25% deposits offer preferential interest rates.

- Expect to pay slightly higher interest rates via Limited Company applications (~1% higher).

- If you are buying via a Limited Company, it is commonplace for lenders to request for a personal guarantee to be signed.

- Expect to pay a valuation and application fee to the lender. (Prices vary between lenders £250+)

- There is usually a minimum property value stated by the lender - Can go as low as £50,000 though.

- Be aware that some lenders will restrict lending on certain types of non standard property construction and certain tenant types.

- If you are planning to fully refurbish a property, prior to letting it, mortgage lending is not considered appropriate by most lenders and you may be better to look at Bridging Finance. Be aware of all the additional costs that come with this type of lending.

- If you can afford to buy the property in cash and then refinance after completing a refurbishment, most mortgage lenders require that the property has been owned for 6 months prior to application for a mortgage.

Using B2L Mortgages

Understanding how to us B2L mortgage products is a powerful and necessary piece of knowledge when looking to create a property investment portfolio. These are the generic guidelines that I have found to be applicable to nearly all the different lenders, but these are by no means comprehensive as there is always a subtle difference between each lender.

Broadly speaking, it is possible to purchase or remortgage a B2L property with up to 80% LTV (Loan To Value) of the actual purchase price (or valuation for remortgages). Typically there are products offered for 75% and 60% LTV by most lenders and the lower the LTV, the lower the interest rates applied. In reality, I prefer 75% LTV as these products typically have competitive rates and fees associated with them, as well as minimising the amount of capital deposit required.

It is commonplace for the best rates to usually require a fixed period of 2-5 years but will often have an ERC (Early Repayment Charge) applicable. This is usually a percentage of the outstanding mortgage balance, dependent on the remaining number of years of the fixed portion of the mortgage. Note that the fixed term is not the total term of the mortgage i.e. A 2 year fixed rate product is typically a 25 year mortgage with a fixed interest rate for the first 2 years and then reverts to the lenders much higher SVR (standard Variable Rate) of interest for the remaining 23 years. Once the fixed period has ended it is preferable to switch to another mortgage product with a lower rate than the SVR i.e a remortgage. This can be with the same or different lender of your choice.

Variable rate products have no ERC but often higher interest rates.

Limited Company B2L mortgage products have ~1% higher rates and expect a product fee of £1000+ (can be added to mortgage), as a rule of thumb.

Most (not all!) lenders require the applicant to have a minimum gross earnings of £25,000/yr and most will not take declared rental income into account here.

The property rental income will be stress tested to help satisfy the lender that the mortgage will be paid. This is a calculation which involves applying a 5-6% interest rate to the amount borrowed. Then, the expected rent must be more than 1.25 times the stressed interest rate for lower rate (20%) tax payers and Limited Companies or 1.45 times the stressed interest rate for higher rate (40-45%) tax payers.

The property should be in a rentable condition with EPC (Energy Performance Certificate) rating between A-E. More lenders are now specifically asking for this.

Remortgages and equity release products have the same above conditions but can only be used once the property has been owned for 6+ months.

Remember that equity released through remortgaging is tax free!

If property is worth more than when it was initially purchased, through capital appreciation over time or forced appreciation as result of refurbishment, these products enable investors to recycle their initial capital deposit. As lenders will usually allow 75% LTV of the new higher value of the property.

<u>Be aware of portfolio landlord criteria</u>:

4+ B2L properties is the usual criteria for lenders.

Lenders usually ask for information about your whole portfolio when applying for any new mortgage product. This includes remortgaging an owned property with a new lender.

A Total Portfolio LTV > 75% will restrict your lending options and if there is a lender, they would usually increase the fees and interest rates.

Lenders will also look to stress test the whole portfolio when deciding whether or not to lend. This is usually 125% of the monthly interest repayment, assuming a 5-6% interest rate on the amount borrowed.

Aiming to reduce your overall portfolio LTV is a worthwhile consideration over time. Interest only mortgages dictate that the capital debt is not being repaid each month but it is possible to decide to overpay periodically when/if you choose. This is usually up 10% of the remaining balance in any given year for fixed rate products, without charges from the lender.

As property values increase over years (historically correct for the last 1000 years or so), the LTV of any property will decrease assuming no further equity released after initial capital repaid.

It is worth thinking about how to reduce the LTV of a portfolio. One could pay back a bit of each mortgage in turn or just focus on paying down the whole of one mortgage? There are benefits to both. The first option would eventually allow access to cheaper mortgage rates for each property, therefore increasing the cash flow of the portfolio. The second option is my preferred choice as it allows a few other options, in addition to reducing the overall portfolio LTV. Firstly, once the property is fully owned (unencumbered), the owner is no longer restricted by any lender conditions. Secondly, an unencumbered property is an asset that can be used as collateral when accessing other forms of lending such as bridging finance. This may allow other investing strategies to be developed over time. Finally, it is a lot easier to sell one unencumbered property to raise a significant amount of capital if needed and this alone is useful when deciding how to protect a portfolio from the risk of property prices crashing.

It is also worth noting that if a portfolio has 75% LTV and there is a property market crash that wipes out 25% of all property values. Then the likely-hood is that any refinance may be based on lower values and as such 75% of the lower valued property (75% of initial value) means that the investor will not be able to refinance to the same level. As such, easier access to capital from an unencumbered property becomes advantageous in enabling the investor to reduce other mortgages accordingly. It also potentially allows an investor to purchase property quickly during such a downturn. It is therefore beneficial to consider a mix of fixed products of various different lengths as well as repaying some capital periodically as a pragmatic approach to strengthen your portfolio from such a risk, which is my preferred strategy.

Buy, Refurbish, Remortgage (BRR)

Using the knowledge of how B2L mortgages work is the more interesting part. Theoretically, it is possible to purchase a property at a discount from its true value. This is usually possible because the seller (vendor) is in a situation whereby, selling at a discount is preferable to not selling at all. Buying quickly, in cash is a major advantage to the vendor in these situations as you can remove the doubt of a sale falling through. Once you find these types of vendors, this strategy becomes more effective. Specifically, we also want to look for similar type and sized properties in the local area with their actual sale prices (Rightmove Sold or Land Registry). This means we can be confident in the value of the discount. Once the property has been purchased, we ideally want to refurbish the property to improve it in as many ways as possible. This is important because we want to be able to prove the improvements have increased the value of he property alongside comparable sale values to assist in the next step. Remortgaging the property once the refurbishment is complete (usually >6 months after purchase) will require a valuer from the lender to assess the property. It is at this point we want to show the evidence of works done and local comparable sales prices in the area to justify the increase in value. Then, it becomes possible to remortgage up to 75-80% of the new value of the property. Ideally, all of the capital spent will be returned as a result of the refinance, and the property will give a monthly cashflow on top. With all your money back in your pocket, simply rinse and repeat as many times as you want to.

Worked Example (Theoretical):

True value of property	£100,000
Purchase Price	£70,000
Solicitor Fee	£850
Stamp Duty Land Tax (3%)	£2,100
Light Refurbishment Costs	£2,000
Total Cost	£74,950

Re-valuation at 6 months from date of purchase £100,000

Mortgage (Interest Only) Loan to Value (LTV) of 75%

Equity Released is £75,000

Thus, all the initial capital invested is returned and a 25% equity is created in the property as well as a recurring monthly rental income.

Real Example:

RICS Valuation prior to purchase £50,000

Purchase price £39,999 (cash)

Solicitor Fee £850

Stamp Duty Land Tax £0 (property purchases < £40,000 are exempt of Additional Dwelling Supplement, ADS)

Light Refurbishment £3,000

Total Cost £43,849

Re-valuation at 6 months from date of purchase £50,000

Mortgage (Interest Only) Loan to Value (LTV) of 75%

Equity Released is	£37,500
Rental profit for 6 months	£2,500
Capital left in deal at 6 months	£3,849
Equity created in 6 months	£12,500

Over 6 months, the rental profit has repaid the remaining capital left in the deal and this property is effectively an infinite return on investment as all the capital has been returned. The added bonus is that, over time the capital value of the property will increase, but ultimately it does not necessarily impact the overall return on investment. As it is possible to own this type of property for decades, at the end of the mortgage term, I would have the choice to pay the small mortgage value to the lender or sell the property as a means to repay the mortgage balance. But as it is possible to follow this example through a company structure, there is no defined date at which the company must sell, as it is possible for a company to refinance a property even if I was over 100 years old, as the company owns the property, not an individual.

Once this strategy can be used effectively, it then becomes possible to buy properties using other investor finance. In fact, the example that I described above, was paid for, using another investors £40,000. This meant that I was able to invest in this property with much less of my own capital as well as being confident to offer the investor a guaranteed return on their investment. Because I was able to offer the investor all their initial funds back within 7 months, they decided that they wanted me to re-invest the money again and continue to pay them a % return on their money that was way above anything they could achieve in a savings account.

This meant I was able to own a property, create equity and a recurring rental income with less than £4,000 of savings. And it has been the method that I have used repeatedly to acquire a sizeable property portfolio with a fraction of the upfront capital needed.

Get the Property Ready to Rent

Congratulations, you now own a buy to let investment property! Now we need to get it suitable for the target tenants. All rental properties will require standard checks prior to letting. If you are using an agent (which I would recommend), they should keep you up to date with the legal requirements of landlords.

All rental properties will need the following:

- Gas Safety Certificate (annually if gas supplied to the property)
- Carbon Monoxide detector (if gas supplied to the property)
- Smoke alarms - preferably mains electricity connected

- Fire alarms - preferably mains integrated

- Electrical Installation Condition Report (5 yearly or between change of tenants)

- PAT certificate (Portable Appliance Testing) of any appliances provided by Landlord (e.g. fridge freezer / Washing machine etc, basically anything with a plug)

- Legionella Risk Assessment

- EPC (Energy Performance Certificate) rating within the last 10 years (Currently E or above but this is expected to be increased to C and above in the coming years)

- Landlord Licence (varies between councils, mandatory in Scotland and N. Ireland)

- Landlord Insurance & Buildings Insurance are essential.

- Rent guarantee insurance is optional, but statistically less important as the portfolio grows because the probability of none payment of rent causing cash flow difficulties decreases (Risk of 1 property = 100%, 2 properties = 50%, 3 properties = 33%, 4 properties = 25% …… etc).

- Get the property cleaned and ready for marketing photographs and virtual tour.

- Virtual tours are becoming increasingly common with agents asking prospective tenants to view online and in some cases go through tenant referencing checks prior to a physical viewing of the property.

There are numerous tenant checks (referencing, employment, right to rent etc) that should be completed prior to renting a property, as well as undertaking an appropriate inventory of the property and setup of the appropriate tenancy agreement. The additional amount of time that it will take to conduct viewings which adhere to social distancing will undoubtably make any payment to a reputable letting agent be completely worthwhile. Most letting agents offer a tenant find (fixed fee) or full management service (~10% of gross rent). I prefer to utilise a full management service as it provides an initial contact barrier between myself and the tenant as well as the expertise of an agent when the tenant does not pay rent. In practice, I only have to deal with a few agents instead of multiple tenants.

In 8 years, I have only had to evict one tenant for non payment of rent (< 5% of all tenancies issued) and I am grateful for the work that my agent undertook on my behalf, to obtain legal access to the property but also orchestrate the process of claiming the unpaid arrears from that same tenant, via the courts.

In what could have been a very stressful situation, I effectively had to write a few emails for it to be sorted and unfortunately it did take well over 18 months in total, which is not uncommon. I certainly do not object to a good agent, getting paid for doing a good job, finding and looking after my tenants professionally, as well as protecting my privacy and property. When you find a good agent, the time and effort they save is priceless!

Maintaining the Property

Regular maintenance is to be expected by every landlord and it is up to you to decide if you are happy to allow the managing agent to appoint their contractors or whether you would prefer your own. Either way is fine, both have their merits and regardless, I would expect to be contacted by the managing agent for maintenance queries raised by the tenant or as a result of a routine inspection. As a rule of thumb, anticipating 5-10% of gross rent, or having a rainy day fund of £X (only you can decide this figure) is prudent to cover any potential maintenance costs per property or for the whole portfolio. If you are planning on creating a portfolio, then you may consider getting to know local tradespeople that you trust and you may also find that some tradespeople can do multiple trades which is very useful. As your portfolio grows, there are certainly savings to be negotiated with economies of scale.

I used to get a feeling of dread every time the phone rang or I saw an email from the letting agent, that there was something wrong and no doubt costly, with one of my properties. Over the years I have learnt, realised and now appreciate these same calls and emails. This is partly because there are recurring themes which I am more familiar at dealing with, but also because these are issues that allow an informal opportunity to inspect the property as well as ensure the property remains up to date and tenanted for the years ahead by fixing problems early. Thus avoiding potentially massive repairs and costs. Interestingly, on separate occasions, as a result of discussing communal building repairs, I have been able to buy a flat at a discounted price directly from another landlord as well as being approached to sell a property to another landlord.

The majority of my portfolio is fully managed by professional letting agents, however over time, I have acquired a number of contacts for local tradespeople who I can rely on when needed. As such, when I am informed of any issues at a property, I am able to instruct my own tradesperson or decide to utilise the contacts of the letting agent. In the majority of instances, I have found that my own tradespeople are generally more cost effective and responsive to most maintenance requests. The added advantage of using my own tradespeople is that over time, they have seen the same properties on multiple occasions, giving them a historical knowledge prior to any current issue as well as being able to take a proactive approach to the problems highlighted by the tenant. This has become easier with time and trust, between myself and each tradesperson but it ultimately saves us all time, effort and cost. They are also able to highlight if the tenant is looking after the property as a result of their unplanned visit which can be rather insightful in some cases.

These are the most common maintenance issues that seem to occur and can be reasonably expected at some point, regardless of the type, size or style of property:

The Boiler does not work.

Regardless of the type (Gas/Wet Electric/Oil) or manufacturer, this is a predictable maintenance concern for landlords and tenants, and the age of the boiler is often the first red flag. Older boilers (>20yrs) are more prone to issues and their parts are often more difficult to find as well as expensive when you do. It may be beneficial to consider a regular servicing and parts plan for older style boilers as long as it is feasible compared to the cost of replacement. A reputable heating engineer should be able to advise where appropriate.

A common situation when any new tenant moves into a property with a gas combination boiler is that the heating will not work as a result of low water pressure or the pilot light is out (usually as a result of the heating not being used during the void period). These are easy to resolve and the tenant can be instructed by the letting agent on how to solve the problem themselves.
A leaking radiator valve can also cause a loss of pressure and this does require a tradesperson competent with basic plumbing to fix and therefore reduce the potential for water damage as well as preventing the tenant from inadvertently over pressurising the boiler (which can lead to further problems).

Water leaking through the ceiling:

Water damage can be expensive to repair as well as potentially disruptive for the tenant. Identifying and resolving a small leak is preferable to a larger one. I have had this same issue in houses and flats and on each occasion, the key has been to identify the source of the leak. Places to be aware of (but not limited to):

- Blocked drains/gutters
- Slipped tiles on roof

- Defective lead flashing around chimney stacks
- Defective pointing/masonry/window casing
- Overflowing water tanks
- Concealed, defective pipework
- Defective sealant around bath or shower tray

Whatever the source of the leak, adequate inspection and resolution from a suitable specialist is the most cost effective option, as a cheap temporary repair is always followed by a more expensive definitive solution eventually.

Bathroom:

Issues relating to the toilet being blocked, not flushing or flushing constantly are usually reported rather quickly by tenants and can be easily rectified by a tradesperson with basic plumbing skills. Toilet flush mechanisms do not last forever, so these are not unreasonable to replace as necessary. Tenant education about what they can and cannot flush down the toilet is often required and given at the start of their tenancy if appropriate (macerating toilets, septic tanks etc). However, for my tenants, the first call out for this issue is reasonable but subsequent blockages are their responsibility to resolve, especially if they have ignored previous information given to them.

Electric showers are a great option for rental properties that have gas combo boilers, as the tenant can still use the shower even if the boiler is not working. Unfortunately they also have a tendency to breakdown and require replacement after 5+ years. When replacing any electric shower, it is helpful to know the make and model of the previous shower, as manufacturers tend to keep the water inlet and wall fixing holes in the same place on newer models, making it simpler to install the new model. However, be aware of the electrical capacity of the new model as it may require more power than the current wire installed in the bathroom and therefore not work properly. Again, a reputable tradesperson (plumber or electrician) should be able to advise accordingly.

Defective or leaking bath/shower tray sealant is straightforward to replace and can significantly reduce the possibility of significant water damage to the room or flat below. Any experienced handyman or tradesperson can fix this, but be aware that it is their time that is the significant cost for any such repair. I usually recommend easily available anti-mould sprays to the tenants as this prevents the unsightly black mould build up, which can then lead to defective seals over time.

Kitchen:

Sealant behind kitchen sinks and taps is the most common place to find water damage in the kitchen. Over time, this can result in significant damage to the kitchen worktop which will eventually need to be fully replaced. As such, it is more cost effective to replace and maintain the sealant than replace a full kitchen work surface and this is an important part of any regular inspection of the property.

Any appliances that are provided as part of the tenancy are the responsibility of the landlord to maintain. It is therefore preferable to provide the minimum number of appliances where possible as they will eventually breakdown. In reality, it may be necessary to rent the property with appliances as this can be common in some areas. It is helpful to know where to obtain specialist help for repairing appliances that are salvageable but beyond their guarantee period. However, it is possible to gain tax relief if a replacement appliance is required, and most online retailers can install the new appliance and remove/recycle the old one too.

Decoration:

Damp (mould) staining on wall is a troublesome problem in particular. Any rising damp should be checked for prior to purchasing the property and dealt with accordingly if necessary. More often than not, the issue of damp (mould) staining is as a result of poor ventilation and heating of the property. This is particularly marked in red brick terraced houses c1900-1920. The solution is through education of tenants and advising them to open a window especially when drying clothes on radiators, or purchase a dehumidifier. This prevents the accumulation of warm damp air within the property and subsequent staining on the walls.

I have no objection to tenants asking if they can paint a room(s) within the property as long as they are willing to repaint the original neutral colour prior to when they wish to leave. It is apparent that those tenants who do ask this, are most likely to stay in the property for longer than 2 years and look after the property as it is their home. I would be delighted if every tenant wanted to ask this question!

Summary

Start with your end goal in mind and spend time doing your research before you buy any property. Make sure you buy at the best price to allow the investment to work as intended and utilise other peoples time and expertise to ensure that you don't inadvertently create a whole new job with unnecessary stresses. Treat your property investments as if you were selling a product and respect your tenants, as they are your customers and you can generate a lifelong *almost* passive income, as well as benefit from capital increases in property values. If I can be of any help to you, please feel free to contact me at info@wickhamproperty.co.uk or visit my property investing blog at www.wickhamproperty.co.uk.

Best of luck with your B2L property investments.

About the Author

Matthew started investing in B2L residential property in 2013 at the age of 27, whilst living and working full time as a doctor in Glasgow. Over the past 8 years, he has re-invested rental profits to build a property portfolio with a GDV > £1M (14 separate properties valued between £12,000 - £210,000) and currently owns B2L property in England, Scotland and Northern Ireland. He is the first to admit he has made mistakes along the way, but thankfully property investing can be forgiving with time and the real learning is in the 'doing better next time'.

Where possible he is keen to help others to learn how to build their own property investment portfolio and regularly writes articles for his blog at www.wickhamproperty.co.uk.

Printed in Great Britain
by Amazon

76480308R00031